MW00716386

LifeGuide® FAMILY Bible Studies

for Parents and Kids to Do Together

Good Choice, Bad Choice

18 Studies on Making Good Decisions

With Notes for Parents

Darrel A. Trulson

General Editor
James C. Galvin, Ed.D.

InterVarsity Press
Downers Grove, Illinois 60515, USA

Crossway Books
Leicester, UK

InverVarsity Press
P.O. Box 1400, Downers Grove, IL 60515, USA

Crossway Books
38 De Montfort Street, Leicester LE1 7GP, UK

© 1995 by The Livingstone Corporation

All rights reserved. No part of this book may be reproduced in any form without written permission from the publisher.

InterVarsity Press®, U.S.A., is the book-publishing division of InterVarsity Christian Fellowship®, a student movement active on campus at hundreds of universities, colleges and schools of nursing in the United States of America, and a member movement of the International Fellowship of Evangelical Students. For information about local and regional activities, write Public Relations Dept., InterVarsity Christian Fellowship, 6400 Schroeder Rd., P.O. Box 7895, Madison, WI 53707-7895.

LifeGuide® is a registered trademark of InterVarsity Christian Fellowship.

All Scripture quotations are from the International Children's Bible, New Century Version, *copyright © 1986, 1988, 1994 by Word Publishing, Dallas, Texas 75039. Used by permission.*

This book was developed exclusively for InterVarsity Press by The Livingstone Corporation. James C. Galvin, Daryl J. Lucas and Linda R. Joiner, project staff.

Cover photograph: Michael Goss

Activities: Deborah Peska-Keiser

USA ISBN 0-8308-1114-1
UK ISBN 1-85684-133-2

Printed in the United States of America ♾

26	25	24	23	22	21	20	19	18	17	16	15	14	13	12	11	10	9	8	7	6	5	4	3	2	1
17	16	15	14	13	12	11	10	09	08	07	06	05	04	03	02	01	00	99	98	97	96	95			

CONTENTS

Welcome to LifeGuide® Family Bible Studies

If you have ever wondered how to make Bible study fun for kids, you will be delighted with this series of study guides. It provides an easy way to study the Bible with a young child or all together as a family. LifeGuide® Family Bible Studies were created especially for families with children ages 4-12. The simple, friendly format makes it easy for adults and children to finish together in just fifteen minutes a day. The material is undated so you can work through the guide at your own pace and according to your family's schedule.

Getting the Most from LifeGuide® Family Bible Studies

Understanding the format used in this series allows you to adapt each lesson to the needs of your family. Each lesson includes a passage from the Bible to read together, questions to discuss, fun activities and a prayer. You can spend more time on some sections and less on others, depending on the age and needs of your child.

Opening. When you sit down together, you need some way to focus your child's attention. The introductory paragraphs start with the child's frame of reference and leads him or her to the truth presented in the Bible passage. Often, the opening includes a question to ask your child or family so that you can find out more about what they are thinking. The opening also creates interest in the Bible verses for that lesson. If your child can read, have him or her read both the opening and the Bible text.

Bible Reading. The translation used in these study guides is the *International Children's Bible*. Having the text reprinted in the study guides makes it easy to use, and also allows children to use highlighters and colored pencils in their study of the Scriptures without fear of ruining a Bible. If you prefer, you can easily use other Bibles in conjunction with the lesson. Either way, the Bible reading usually generates questions.

Discussion Questions. Each lesson includes several questions to discuss to deepen your understanding of the passage. Some of the questions will require your child to look for the answers in the Bible reading. Others will help your child to think about how the truths apply to life.

✎More difficult questions for older children are marked with a pencil.

Activity. Each study guide contains a variety of fun paper and pencil activities such as simple crossword puzzles, mazes and decoding games. These activities can help motivate kids to complete the lesson each day. If you are sharing one study guide with several children, you can take turns letting each child complete the puzzle for the day.

Prayer. The main point of the lesson is also expressed in the prayer that you and your child can pray

Prayer. The main point of the lesson is also expressed in the prayer that you and your child can pray together. You can add more to each prayer as appropriate. But your child may not want to stop there.

Bonus. We have also included an active learning experience for a longer session when you have time and your child wants to do more. Or, you may want to save it for another day. The bonus activity provides additional reinforcement for the main point of the lesson.

Notes to Parents. You will find notes conveniently placed in the margins of each lesson rather than in a separate leader's guide. These notes provide practical help as you study the Bible together.

Studying the Bible with Children

You will find it useful to keep developmental differences in mind as you study the Bible together. After all, children are not miniature adults, and they would not learn well from Bible study approaches suitable for adults. The following chart illustrates some of the characteristics of children at different ages and relates them to Bible study. Which have you noticed in your own child?

Ages	Characteristics of Children	Implications for Bible Study
4-5 early childhood	In general, children this age: • learn by asking questions • usually have many fears • sometimes confuse make-believe with reality • have a growing sense of right and wrong • have a relatively short attention span (5-10 minutes)	As you teach your child: • allow them to ask questions, and answer them patiently • discuss God's protection • don't be surprised if Bible stories get mixed up with pretend stories • distinguish between right and wrong • don't expect to finish each lesson in one sitting
6-8 middle childhood	• are emergent readers; some are fluent readers • think concretely and literally; abstractions tend to be difficult • are able to memorize information easily • thrive on approval from their parents	• use this as an opportunity to practice reading skills • discuss the here and now, avoiding abstractions • make a game out of memorizing a few short verses from a study guide • praise and encourage as much as possible
9-11 later childhood	• are beginning to reason more logically • want to be independent learners • eagerly enter into competitive activities • have many questions about Christianity	• use the questions marked with a pencil, which are more challenging to answer • let your child set the pace and read as you facilitate • try not to have a winner and loser of the Bible study • help your child find answers to his or her questions in the Bible

With so many differences between older and younger children, you will have to adapt some lessons and skip certain activities. You may want to encourage the older children to help the younger ones. Think of these lessons as a helpful guide. Answering your child's questions may ultimately be more important than finishing a lesson. The following guidelines will help you adapt the lessons to meet the needs of children of different ages.

Using These Studies as a Family

You can use these studies to guide your family devotions. If you do, the biggest challenge will be keeping the attention and interest of both younger and older children at the same time. One useful technique for leading the discussion is to ask the question, then allow the children to answer one at a time, starting with the youngest and moving in order to the oldest. This way the younger children have a chance to talk, and the older children have a chance to add their answers. Don't let one child be critical of another child's answer. Parents can join in the fun, too. Your children will be interested in the personal applications that you see in the lesson.

You may have to change some of the wording in the lessons. When using the prayer as a family, change the *me* and *my* to *us* and *our*. Also, you may not want to do the puzzle as a group. Above all, keep it fun. Try to end with a snack or treat of some kind. You may find that your family wants to work through the entire series.

Using These Studies with a Younger Child

Younger children have boundless energy and short attention spans. Keep each lesson short and sweet. You may not be able to finish every lesson in one sitting; if so, just finish up the next day. Make use of the bonus activities at the end because these are more active in nature.

In general, don't use the questions marked with a pencil.

Some of the puzzles are designed to appeal to younger children, and some to older children. Feel free to skip the puzzles that seem too difficult.

Allow your child to ask questions at any point in the lesson. Sometimes the questions may seem endless, but that is a sign that your child is learning. Praise and encourage your child as much as possible during the study.

If your child cannot read, read the prayer one phrase at a time and have the child repeat it after you. Encourage your child to express his or her feelings to God in prayer, and also to make requests to his or her Heavenly Father.

If your child is an emergent reader, make the Bible study a fun experience by letting him or her circle important words or use a highlighter (just like Mom and Dad). Colored pens and pencils can add excitement to the lesson. Make Bible study an adventure.

Using These Studies with an Older Child

Older children don't want to be treated like little kids. They will quickly spot the parts of each lesson intended for younger children. If this happens, don't argue. Simply let them know that they will be treated differently, that they don't have to do all the parts of every lesson, and that this study should be very *easy* for them to complete.

In general, skip the bonus activities, because these are primarily for younger children. You can let your child choose whether or not to complete the puzzle in each lesson. Some of them will be far too easy, and some will be a challenge. The discussion questions marked with a pencil are more difficult and are for older children. Don't skip these. You may want to keep a concordance and Bible dictionary handy for questions that come up along the way.

Older children can be challenged to begin a personal devotional life. If appropriate for your child, consider letting him or her work alone on the study as a step toward developing a personal quiet time. Discuss the lesson with your child after he or she has answered all the questions.

The LifeGuide® Family Bible Studies

The entire series includes eight different study guides. Each study guide contains 18 lessons on a particular topic. Start with the topics that would be most interesting to your family.

Super Bible Heroes. The Bible is full of people who did great things, heroic things. But they really aren't very much bigger or stronger or braver than you. Reading their stories, you'll see how God can help you do what seems impossible on your own.

Grown Up on the Inside. Just as food, exercise and rest help us grow up on the outside, the Bible shows us how to grow up on the inside. It shows us how to practice being loyal, humble, honest, respectful and caring—everything that God knows will make us happy and healthy.

Fruit-Filled. Everybody has a favorite: blueberry Pop-Tarts, apple pie, Jell-O with bananas in it. The Bible tells us how we can be filled with God's favorite fruits: love, joy, peace, patience, kindness, goodness, faithfulness, gentleness and self-control.

Good Choice, Bad Choice. Every day we make choices: Will I watch TV or play outside after supper? What will I do when someone makes me mad? The Bible shows us how God helped other people make decisions—and how he will help us.

Jesus Loves Me. Jesus is the friend who never disappoints us or moves to another city. He is the friend who always understands our problems, who always has time to listen and help. The Bible shows us many ways Jesus loves us and helps us see his care in the things that happen to us every day.

The Friendship Factory. Friends make life fun. They help us learn, grow and know God better. And what the Bible says about friendship can help us be better friends to the people we know.

Wisdom Workshop. King Solomon wanted to be wise. So he asked God for wisdom. In the book of Proverbs he tells what God helped him learn about wisdom—and what you can learn too.

God's Great Invention. God made comets and colors and kangaroos. But his greatest invention is people—people like you. The Bible shows how God made you different from everyone else, with gifts and talents to make your own special mark on his world.

No matter which study guide you begin with, you will be introducing your child to the exciting challenge of studying God's Word and planting the seeds for a lifetime habit of personal Bible study.

James C. Galvin
General Editor

1

Jealous Brothers

If needed, take a few moments to explain what jealousy is and give some examples your child can relate to.

When someone else does well and you don't, it's easy to feel jealous. Jealousy is a dangerous sin because it can lead to other sins. Jealousy is often followed by stealing, lying and anger. Whenever we sin by being jealous, we need to ask God to forgive and change us so that we do not sin in other areas as well.

The Bible shows us how terrible and dangerous jealousy can be. In the story of Cain and Abel, two brothers brought gifts to worship God. God accepted one and rejected the other. Cain became jealous. Let's find out what happened.

Bible Reading

As in many stories from the Old Testament, the violence in the story of Cain may be upsetting either to you or to your child. Take some time to discuss the fact that the Bible doesn't hide the fact that human beings are sinful. It also states clearly that this is why God reached out to us, first through the prophets and then through his Son, Jesus Christ— to save us from our sin.

³Cain brought a gift to God. He brought some food from the ground. ⁴Abel brought the best parts of his best sheep. The Lord accepted Abel and his gift. ⁵But God did not accept Cain and his gift. Cain became very angry and looked unhappy. ⁶The Lord asked Cain, "Why are you angry? Why do you look so unhappy? ⁷If you do good, I will accept you. But if you do not do good, sin is ready to attack you. Sin wants you. But you must rule over it." ⁸Cain said to his brother Abel, "Let's go out into the field." So Cain and Abel went into the field. Then Cain attacked his brother Abel and killed him. (Genesis 4:3-8)

Discussion

1. What did Cain and Abel each bring to the Lord (verses 3–4)?

2. What did God say was ready to attack Cain (verse 7)?

3. Why was Cain jealous of Abel?

4. What did God want Cain to do (verse 7)?

5. What are several different ways people can become jealous?

✎6. What sorts of things make you feel jealous? Why?

✎7. Has anyone ever been jealous of you? How did that effect the relationship you had with that person?

2. You may need to explain that God rejected Cain's gift because Cain did not do what was right. He ignored God's instructions and did whatever he wanted to do. That's why it says that "sin is ready to attack you"—Cain always followed his own selfish desires.

5. Answers can include relationships, achievements, money or other possessions.

6. The questions marked with a pencil are more difficult and intended for older children.
   This question may provide a good opportunity to see your child's concrete struggles with materialism. Or, it may lead to a discussion of privileges that come with age—a younger child may be jealous of the opportunities granted to an older child. If you approach this discussion as a fellow sinner, subject to struggles of your own, you will have an excellent opportunity to help your child deal with his or her desires, now and in the future.

Activity

t	1. T.V. __ a b l e
st	2. For a horse __ __ a b l e
f	3. To weaken __ __ __ a b l e
m	4. Something to eat on __ a b l e
c	5. A story __ a b l e
dis	6. A woman's name __ a b e l
l	7. A tag __ a b e l

Use the definitions provided to reveal the words that rhyme with *Abel.* Use the letter combinations on the left to help you.

Prayer

Dear God,
Thank you for all the things you have given me. Please help me not to become jealous of anyone else. Help me to choose to be satisfied with what I have.
In Jesus' name, amen.

Bonus

Have your family put on a play of the story of Cain and Abel. Give each person a part (if necessary, two parts) and start where Abel is a shepherd and Cain is a farmer. You could draw pictures of vegetables and sheep on paper for props. At the end of the play, discuss with your family how God hates jealousy and why it is so destructive.

2

Moses' Mother Obeys God

It is not always easy to obey God. Suppose you know the truth about something bad that other kids want to keep a secret. If you do the right thing and tell an adult, the other kids may get mad.

When Pharaoh told the people to kill their newborn baby boys, Moses' parents obeyed God. God blessed them, and Moses grew up to be a great leader of the people of Israel.

Bible Reading

²²The king commanded all his people: "Every time a baby boy is born to the Hebrews, you must throw him into the Nile River. But let all the girl babies live."

¹There was a man from the family of Levi. He married a woman who was also from the family of Levi. ²She became pregnant and gave birth to a son. She saw how wonderful the baby was, and she hid him for three months. ³But after three months, she was not able to hide the baby any longer. So she got a basket and covered it with tar so that it would float. She put the baby in the basket. Then she put the basket among the tall grass at the edge of the Nile River. . . .

⁶The king's daughter opened the basket and saw the baby boy. He was crying, and she felt sorry for him. She said, "This is

For more details on the story of Moses and his parents, read Exodus 1:8—2:10.

one of the Hebrew babies."

⁷Then the baby's sister asked the king's daughter, "Would you like me to find a Hebrew woman to nurse the baby for you?"

⁸The king's daughter said, "Yes, please." So the girl went and got the baby's own mother. (Exodus 1:22; 2:1-3, 6-8)

Discussion

1. Why did Moses' mother hide her baby (verse 22)?

2. How long did Moses' mother hide him (verse 2)?

3. Why would it be hard to hide a baby for a long time?

4. Who felt sorry for Moses and made sure that he lived (verse 6)?

5. Why was Moses' parents' decision to save their baby boy a good choice?

✎6. Is it easy to obey God's laws? Why or why not?

✎7. How do we know if a particular law in our city or nation is good and should be obeyed?

1. Reassure your child that this will never happen to him or her. Moses' mother lived in a time and country where slavery was common.

4. It may not be clear to young children that the parents hoped that he would be found and rescued. You may need to reassure them that the basket was well-prepared to float. The fact that Moses' sister was waiting nearby to see what happened is another indication that the family was not just abandoning the child.

6. Young children may react initially by saying yes. There is a sense in which God's laws are transparent in their rightness. And, as Jesus said, children are well attuned to the things of the kingdom (Matthew 18:2). Without discouraging their simple loyalty, you may want to give an example of a time when you have had to make a hard choice in relation to obedience to God.

Activity

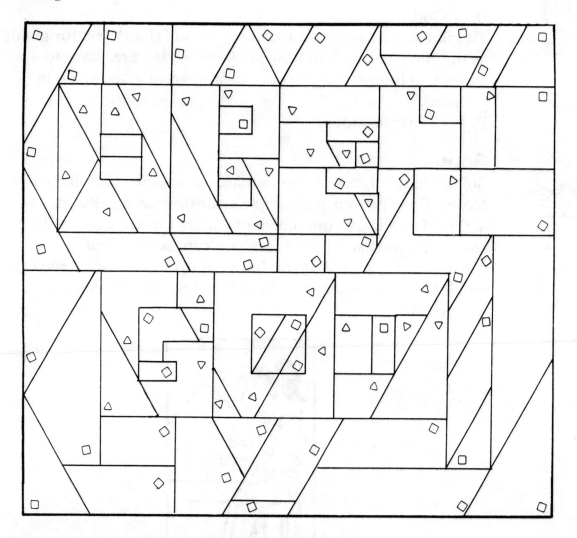

To find a hidden message, color in the shapes that contain a triangle.

Prayer

Dear God,

Thank you that all of your laws are good. Thank you for giving us the Bible to teach us how to obey you. If I ever have to choose, help me to obey your law instead of a law made by people.

In Jesus' name, amen.

Bonus

Build a basket like the one that Moses' mother built for baby Moses. Go with your parent to a craft store and get some wicker. Then weave the pieces of wicker together into a little basket. (If you can't get wicker, you can use strips of construction paper that you have cut up.) You'll soon see how much Moses' mother must have loved him to do so much to save his life!

These stalks were similar to bundles of straw.

3

Rahab Helps God's People

Have you ever played hide-and-seek? It is fun to find new places to hide and see how long it takes someone to find you. But sometimes hiding is frightening. When Rahab protected the spies, she hid them under stalks of flax. Rahab risked her life because she believed in the power of God.

Bible Reading

[4][Rahab] said, "They did come here. But I didn't know where they came from. [5]In the evening, when it was time to close the city gate, they left. I don't know where they went. Go quickly. Maybe you can catch them." [6](But the woman had taken the men up to the roof. She had hidden them there under stalks of flax. She had spread the flax out there to dry.) [7]So the king's men went out looking for the spies from Israel. They went to the places where people cross the Jordan River. The city gate was closed just after the king's men left the city. . . .

[9][Rahab] said, "I know the Lord has given this land to your people. [10]You frighten us very much. Everyone living in this land is terribly afraid of you. . . .

[11]"This is because the Lord your God rules the heavens above and the earth below! [12]So now, make me a promise

If your child is interested in the whole story of Rahab and the spies, you can read Joshua 2:1-24 together.

before the Lord. Promise that you will show kindness to my family just as I showed you kindness." . . .

[14][The men said], "We will trade our lives for your lives. Don't tell anyone what we are doing. When the Lord gives us our land, we will be kind to you. You may trust us." (Joshua 2:4-7, 9-12, 14)

Discussion

1. When have you hidden something so no one would find it?

2. What did Rahab tell the king's men about the spies (verses 4-5)?

3. Where did the king's men go looking for the spies (verse 7)?

4. What did Rahab ask the spies to promise her (verse 12)?

✎5. How did Rahab's choice help to save her and her family?

6. Rahab believed that God was alive and would continue to give the people of Israel success.

6. How did Rahab show her faith in God?

7. This is a difficult moral question that has confronted people in wartime for generations. You may be surprised at the answers and discussion this generates.

✎7. Was Rahab correct for telling a lie to protect the spies? If not, what should she have done?

Activity

God

_ _ _ _ _ the

_ _ _ _ _ _

_ _ _ _ _ and

the _ _ _ _ _

_ _ _ _ _ .

Start at the arrow and write every other letter on the wheel in the blanks. Go around twice. Complete the sentence and discover a truth about God.

Prayer

Dear God,
Please help me to have faith like Rahab did. Help me to believe in your power and greatness even if it means taking big risks. Thank you that you can protect me and keep me safe from harm.
In Jesus' name, amen.

Bonus

Gather your family for a game of hide-and-seek. You can play in the house, in the yard, or at a park. When it is your turn to hide, think about the spies who hid from the enemy soldiers. When the game is over, talk with your family about how Rahab and the spies showed they were brave.

4

Samson Picks a Bad Friend

Allow your child to tell about a time this happened.

Have you ever done something even though you knew it was wrong? Most of us have. Sometimes bad people tell us to do bad things. This happened to Samson when he told Delilah the secret of his strength.

Bible Reading

[16][Delilah] kept bothering Samson about his secret day after day. He become so tired of it he felt he was going to die!

[17]So he told her everything. He said, "I have never had my hair cut. I have been set apart to God as a Nazirite since I was born. If someone shaved my head, then I would lose my strength. I would become as weak as any other man."

[18]Delilah saw that he had told her everything sincerely. So she sent a message to the kings of the Philistines. She said, "Come back one more time. He has told me everything." So the kings of the Philistines came back to Delilah. They brought the silver they had promised to give her. [19]Delilah got Samson to go to sleep. He was lying in her lap. Then she called in a man to shave off the seven braids of Samson's hair. In this way she began to make him weak. And Samson's strength left him. (Judges 16:16-19)

If your child is interested in the whole story, you can read Judges 16:4-22 together.

Discussion

1. What was special about Samson from the time he was born (verse 17)?

2. What did the kings of the Philistines promise to give Delilah if she told them Samson's secret (verse 18)?

3. What should Samson have done when Delilah bothered him for the secret?

4. Samson didn't pick his friends very well. What kinds of bad things do friends sometimes want us to do?

5. The role of someone who cajoles and convinces us to do something we shouldn't is a concept which is likely to be familiar to most children. Your child may need your help or support in dealing with a bad influence, either now or in the future.

5. What are some bad influences that may cause us to disobey God?

6. Although this was only part of Samson's problem, it is a dilemma familiar to young children. You may want to talk with your child about times when secrets are "fun" and times when they are very important.

✎6. What makes it difficult to keep a secret?

✎7. What are some things you can do to resist temptation from others?

Activity

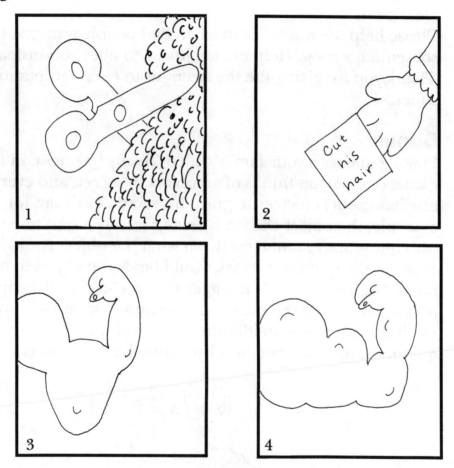

Unscramble these pictures to tell the story of Samson and Delilah. Write the numbers of each picture in the correct order below.

_____   _____   _____   _____

Prayer

Dear God,
Please help me not to listen when bad people want me to do something wrong. Help me to choose to obey you instead. Thank you for giving me the strength to resist temptation. Amen.

Bonus

Play a game with your family called *Twenty Questions.* In this game, one person thinks of an object in secret, and everyone else has twenty chances to guess his secret. Let's say, for example, the object chosen is "swing set." It is best to begin with questions that narrow down what the object could be. Some of the questions to ask would be: Is the object in our house? Can we eat it? Is it bigger than a chair? and so on. The person answering the questions can only respond with yes or no. If no one is able to identify the object within twenty questions, then the person who chose the object wins.

5

Jonathan Protects David

We all enjoy having true friends. True friends stick together and help each other through difficult situations. Who is your true friend?

Jonathan was faced with a difficult situation. His father, Saul, wanted to kill his best friend, David. Saul knew that God had appointed David to be the next king of Israel. Saul wanted David dead so his own son Jonathan could become king after he died. Would Jonathan disobey God and help his father kill David, or would he give up his chance to be king and protect his friend?

Allow your child to respond.

It is important to add that God is our best friend. He demonstrated his love and friendship to us by sending his own Son to die for our sins.

Bible Reading

[12]Jonathan said to David, "I promise this before the Lord, the God of Israel: At this same time day after tomorrow, I will find out how my father feels. If he feels good toward you, I'll send word to you. I'll let you know. [13]But my father may mean to hurt you. If so, I will let you know and send you away safely. May the Lord punish me terribly if I don't do this. And may the Lord be with you as he has been with my father. [14]But show me the kindness of the Lord as long as I live. Do this so that I may not die. [15]You must not stop showing your kindness to my family. Don't do this, even when the Lord has destroyed all your enemies from the earth." (1 Samuel 20:12-15)

If your child is interested in reading more about Jonathan and David, read 1 Samuel 20:1-42.

Discussion

1. What did Jonathan say he was going to find out (verse 12)?

2. Who did Jonathan decide to help, David or Saul (verse 13)?

3. What can you do to become a better friend?

4. What did Jonathan want David to do for him (verses 14-15)?

5. How have you shown your best friend that you like him or her?

6. In order not to inadvertently create a precedent for evaluation of your parental choices and disobedience, you may want to emphasize that Jonathan, the son, was a grown man in this story. Also, his father was clearly disobeying God by wanting to commit murder. Jonathan was choosing to obey God rather than humans.

✎6. Why was Jonathan right to warn David, even though Saul was his father?

7. It can be helpful for your child to have the chance to reflect from time to time on the value of his or her friendships. Otherwise, he or she will most likely take them for granted on a day-to-day basis. If your child is in a relationship which concerns you because it is not wholesome and reciprocal, this might be an opportunity to talk about it and begin to seek out more appropriate companions.

✎7. How has your friend helped you or been kind to you in the past?

Activity

D	E	S	T	R	O	Y	E	D	I
P	P	R	O	G	L	I	V	E	S
H	W	R	T	D	O	E	C	T	R
T	O	M	O	R	R	O	W	E	A
R	H	G	W	M	D	S	D	O	E
A	S	O	Y	L	I	M	A	F	L
E	N	E	M	I	E	S	E	N	D
K	M	K	I	N	D	N	E	S	S

Find the following words from the Scripture reading in the diagram above.
Words may appear vertically, horizontally or diagonally.

promise   God   tomorrow   send   me   kindness   family   enemies
Lord   Israel   good   know   how   live   destroyed   earth

Prayer

Dear God,
Thank you for the friends you have given me. Help me to make
good choices about my friends. Thank you, God, that you are
my best friend. Thank you for all the wonderful things you
have done for me. Help me to love you more and more.
In Jesus' name, amen.

Bonus

Decide on something special you can do to show love to a good
friend this week. Perhaps you can write a note to your friend,
call him or her on the phone, or visit a park together. When
you are with your friend, be sure to say thank you for ways he or
she has been a friend to you.

6

David Spares Saul's Life

If you knew someone was trying to hurt you and you had the perfect chance to hurt that person first, would you do it? That is a hard question, because it is easy to want to pay people back for the mean things they do.

David once faced this very question. King Saul had been trying to kill David for some time; however, when David had the chance to kill Saul, he just cut off a piece of his robe. David trusted the Lord to protect him.

Bible Reading

[4]The men said to David, "Today is the day the Lord talked about! The Lord told you, 'I will give your enemy to you. You can do anything you want with him.' "

Then David crawled near Saul. He cut off a corner of Saul's robe. But Saul did not notice him. [5]Later David felt guilty because he had cut off a corner of Saul's robe. [6]He said to his men, "May the Lord keep me from doing such a thing to my master! Saul is the Lord's appointed king. I should not do anything against him, because he is the Lord's appointed king!" [7]David used these words to stop his men. He did not let them attack Saul. Then Saul left the cave and went his way. (1 Samuel 24:4-7)

If your child is interested in hearing the whole story of Saul chasing David, see 1 Samuel 24:1-22.

Discussion

1. Who thought David should hurt Saul when he had the chance (verse 4)?

2. What did David do that Saul didn't even notice (verse 4)?

3. Why did David say it would be wrong to hurt Saul (verse 6)?

4. This question may elicit some strong feelings, especially if the incident that comes to mind is fairly fresh in your child's memory. If you recall an incident a little farther removed, you may want to remind your child of the details in order to draw a lesson from his or her experience.

4. When have you wanted to pay someone back for something he or she did to you?

5. It is important that children understand that foregoing human vengeance, as David did, does not imply that God does not care that someone has been wronged or hurt. Children can be helped to see that letting an all-powerful God deal with someone is much better than acting upon our own hurt and anger.

5. If someone has been mean to you, how does God want you to treat him or her? Why?

✎6. When have you relied on God's protection in a hurtful situation?

✎7. Why is it a better idea to let God deal with the people who hurt you rather than taking matters into your own hands?

Activity

OREB   __ __ __ __

MYEEN   __ __ __ __ __

ALSU   __ __ __ __

TENAPIPDO   __ __ __ __ __ __ __ __ __

EMTSAR   __ __ __ __ __ __

VAEC   __ __ __ __

YILGUT   __ __ __ __ __ __

Unscramble the letters on the left to reveal words from the Bible reading. When the letters are unscrambled, a word will appear in the column going up and down that describes how we are to treat each other.

Prayer

Dear God,
Please help me not to return evil for evil. Help me to choose to trust you for protection. When people are mean to me, help me to love them instead of hurting them back.
In Jesus' name, amen.

Bonus

Around the supper table, give each person a chance to tell about chances they had to "get even" with someone. Ask them what they did and why. Then ask how God wants us to handle these times.

7

Solomon's Big Wish

Allow your child to respond.

If you could wish for anything in the world, what would it be? Some people want money or friends. Others may wish for power or greatness. When God asked Solomon what he wanted, he asked for wisdom. This request pleased God so much that he also gave Solomon riches and honor. Solomon made a good choice because he thought about God and others before himself.

Bible Reading

[5]While [Solomon] was at Gibeon, the Lord came to him in a dream during the night. God said, "Ask for anything you want. I will give it to you."

[6]Solomon answered, "You were very kind to your servant, my father David. He obeyed you. He was honest and lived right. And you showed great kindness to him when you allowed his son to be king after him. [7]Lord my God, you have allowed me to be king in my father's place. But I am like a little child. I do not have the wisdom I need to do what I must do. [8]I, your servant, am here among your chosen people. There are too many of them to count. [9]So I ask that you give me wisdom. Then I can rule the people in the right way. Then I will know the difference between right and wrong. Without wisdom, it is

If your child is interested in the whole story of Solomon's dream, read 1 Kings 3:1-15.

impossible to rule this great people of yours."

¹⁰The Lord was pleased that Solomon had asked him for this. (1 Kings 3:5-10)

Discussion

1. How did Solomon learn about the goodness of God (verse 6)?

2. Why did Solomon want wisdom (verses 7-9)?

3. If you had a chance like Solomon's, what might you wish for? Why?

3. If your child wants something odd or bad, resist scolding him or her. Instead, ask why he or she thinks this would be good. An effective teaching opportunity may emerge.

4. Why do rulers need wisdom?

5. Note: Try to focus the discussion on serving God and helping others, rather than on doing well in school.

5. How can wisdom help you in your life?

6. By asking God for wisdom, Solomon showed dependence on God. He showed that he understood his true place in God's world and that he needed God's help to do what he had been given to do.

✎6. Why do you think that asking for wisdom pleased God so much?

✎7. For what situation do you want to ask God for wisdom?

Activity

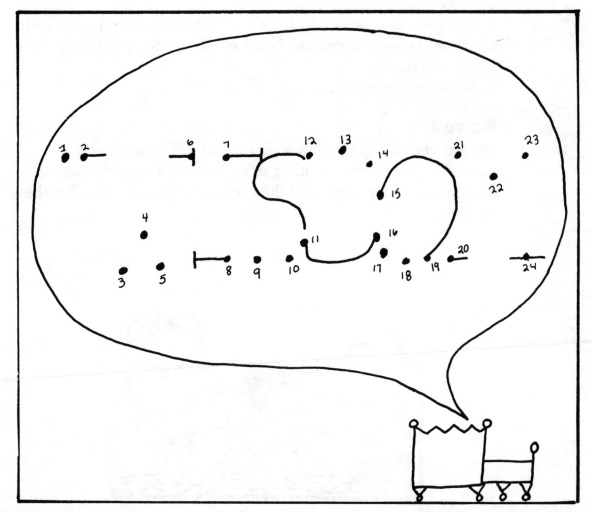

Connect the dots from 1 to 24. You will discover what King Solomon asked God for in a dream.

Prayer

Dear God,

Please give me wisdom to know right from wrong. Please help me to make wise decisions. Help me to ask for the things that make you happy.

In Jesus' name, amen.

Bonus

On a piece of paper, draw a picture of someone doing something wise. On the other side, draw a picture of a person being foolish. Then explain the pictures to your parent, brother or sister.

As a parent, it is good to participate in the same activities as your children. This develops a sense of togetherness with everyone in the family. When an activity calls for drawing a picture like this one, take out your paper and crayons and draw a picture too. Your kids will enjoy seeing your contributions and hearing what you have to say.

⑧ Haman's Evil Plan

Have you ever been very angry with someone? So angry you said, "I hate you"? Hate is a very strong feeling. If we let it stay inside us, it grows until it hurts us.

Haman was a wicked man who thought he was very important. He expected people to bow down and worship him. Mordecai was a Jew who worshiped only God. Haman hated Mordecai.

Give your child a chance to answer. You may want to explain that the only way we can stop hate is to forgive people.

Bible Reading

⁵Haman saw that Mordecai would not bow down to him or kneel before him. And he became very angry. . . . ⁶He thought of himself as too important to try to kill only Mordecai. So he looked for a way to destroy all of Mordecai's people, the Jews, in all of Xerxes' kingdom. . . .

[Queen Esther, a relative of Mordecai, said to the king,] "If it pleases you, let me live. This is what I ask. And let my people live, too. ⁴I ask this because my people and I have been sold to be destroyed. We are to be killed and completely wiped out." . . .⁵ Then King Xerxes asked Queen Esther, "Who is he? Where is he? Who has done such a thing?"

⁶Esther said, "A man who is against us! Our enemy is this wicked Haman!"

⁷The king was very angry [when he heard Haman's plan.] . . .

⁹[Harbona the servant] said, "Look, a platform for hanging people stands near Haman's house. It is 75 feet high. This is the one Haman had prepared for Mordecai." . . .

The king said, "Hang Haman on it!" (Esther 3:5-6; 7:3-7, 9)

Discussion

1. Why did Haman become angry (3:5)?

2. What bad choices did Haman make while he was angry (3:6)?

3. Why was the king angry when he learned what Haman planned to do?

4. Do you think Haman got what he deserved? Why or why not?

5. How can you keep from hating a person who makes you angry?

✎6. What bad things happen when we think we are more important than others?

✎7. How else might Haman have chosen to act when Mordecai wouldn't bow?

5. Children should not come away from this lesson believing that they are never allowed to feel angry. When we feel anger, we still have recourse to prayer; we can take an inner inventory of our attitudes and the reasons for the anger, or we can go to the person who angered us and try to work it out. Haman let his wounded pride fester into hatred and devised a scheme for getting revenge that would have hurt many innocent people.

6. We tend to treat others disrespectfully whenever we think we are more important than they. We may say or do things that hurt them.

7. Haman could have simply accepted it, told Mordecai how he felt, discussed the matter with the king or even forgiven Mordecai. Help your child brainstorm.

Activity

Draw a picture of how you feel and look when you are angry.

Prayer

Dear God,
Thank you for understanding that sometimes I get angry.
Forgive me for the times that I become angry and want to hurt
someone else. Help me to make good choices when I feel angry.
In Jesus' name, amen.

Bonus

Ask a parent to help you with this project in the kitchen. Place
one-fourth cup of vinegar in a tall container (drinking glass,
measuring cup, etc.). Then add one teaspoon of baking soda.
Watch what happens!

What happened in the glass is much like what happens in our
hearts when we let our anger turn into hate. Talk about ways
that you can keep your anger from "boiling over" into hateful
actions

9

Daniel Says No

Allow your child to answer the questions.

What foods do you like to eat? What foods do you prefer to leave on the plate? It's good for children to eat what their parents ask them to.

When Daniel was a teenager, he and many of the people of Israel were captured and taken to the nation of Babylon. The king told them to eat food that God did not want them to have. They were faced with a decision about their food: would they follow God or would they obey the commands of the king? When Daniel and his three friends faced this choice, they came up with a plan that made everyone happy.

Bible Reading

If your child is interested in learning more about Daniel in the king's court, you can read Daniel 1:1-21 together.

[8]Daniel decided not to eat the king's food and wine because that would make him unclean. So he asked Ashpenaz [the guard] for permission not to make himself unclean in this way. . . .

[14]So the guard agreed to test them for ten days. [15]After ten days they looked very healthy. They looked better than all of the young men who ate the king's food. [16]So the guard took away the king's special food and wine. He gave Daniel, Hananiah, Mishael and Azariah vegetables. (Daniel 1:8, 14-16)

Discussion

1. Why did Daniel decide not to eat the king's food (verse 8)?

2. What did the guard give Daniel and his friends to eat instead of the king's food (verse 16)?

3. Why did Daniel have to be brave to ask for a different kind of food?

✎4. If Ashpenaz had not allowed them to eat only clean food, what do you think Daniel and his friends would have done next?

5. Have you ever had to make a choice between following God's ways and following someone else's ideas? What happened?

6. What are some things people tell us to do that go against what God tells us to do?

✎7. When is it good to be picky about what we do? Why?

1. You may need to explain that uncleanness, for Jews, meant disobedience to God's ceremonial law, which told them what foods they could and could not eat. These laws were designed for their own good, physically and spiritually.

3. As slaves, Daniel and his friends had no right to ask for anything. However, they decided to do so because they didn't want to disobey God.

6. People will often encourage us to lie or cheat in certain situations, reasoning that "everybody does it."

7. We should "be picky" about what we do whenever an activity involves something that God has told us to do or not do. That's why Daniel refused to eat the king's food.

Activity

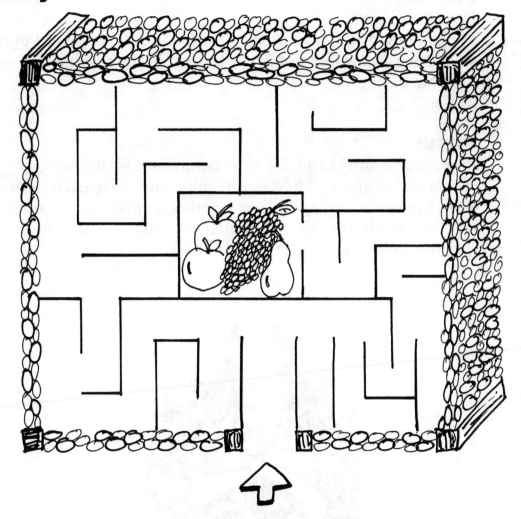

Follow the maze through the king's palace to get to the food that Daniel ate.

Prayer

Dear Lord Jesus,
Please help me to always do what you want. If I am asked to do something you would not like, please help me to make a choice like Daniel did.
Amen.

Bonus

Prepare a healthy snack for your family with fresh fruits, vegetables or grains. Then set the table and serve each person from a plate or tray. As you eat together, explain how Daniel and his friends were healthier than the others even though they didn't eat the king's fancy food.

You may want to take this opportunity to discuss with your child what we know about the foods that are *not* good for us. It may be a new concept for your child that the care of his or her body is important to God.

10

Jesus' Temptation

Allow your child to answer the question.

What is temptation? Temptation is anything that makes us want to do something bad. It is not wrong to be tempted, but it is wrong to give in to the temptation. That is called sin. The best way to fight against temptation is to pray for God's help.

When we are tempted by sin, it is comforting to know that even the Lord Jesus faced temptation. When Jesus was in the desert, the devil tempted him, but Jesus never sinned. Because Jesus was tempted, he understands our struggles and is willing to help us when we face temptation.

Bible Reading

[8]Then the devil led Jesus to the top of a very high mountain. He showed Jesus all the kingdoms of the world and all the great things that are in those kingdoms. [9]The devil said, "If you will bow down and worship me, I will give you all these things."

[10]Jesus said to the devil, "Go away from me, Satan! It is written in the Scriptures, 'You must worship the Lord your God. Serve only him!' "

[11]So the devil left Jesus. And then some angels came to Jesus and helped him. (Matthew 4:8-11)

Discussion

1. What would you do if you saw a big plate of cookies on the table and you knew your mom had said not to touch them?

2. What bad thing was the devil trying to get Jesus to do (verse 9)?

2. Many children will recognize that worshiping the devil was not the right thing for Jesus to choose. Scripture makes it clear that Satan is the Enemy. It is also clear that no one can serve two masters (Matthew 6:24).

✎3. How did the devil make worshiping him seem like a good idea (verses 8-9)?

4. How did the Bible help Jesus answer the devil (verse 10)?

5. For children, as for all of us, choosing not to sin can sometimes be a very difficult decision. It can be useful to point out how appealing the option offered to Jesus was. Seeing through a seemingly good idea and recognizing it as temptation takes many years of practice and much familiarity with the Scriptures.

5. When have you been tempted to do something wrong?

6. What can you do to keep from sinning when you feel tempted?

6. Remind your family that James 4:7 says, "So give yourselves to God. Stand against the devil, and the devil will run away from you."

✎7. How does it help you to know that Jesus also faced difficult temptations?

Activity

Jesus said, "It is written in the Scriptures,

'You $\dfrac{}{10}\ \dfrac{}{3}\ \dfrac{}{15}\ \dfrac{}{7}$

$\dfrac{}{5}\ \dfrac{}{4}\ \dfrac{}{8}\ \dfrac{}{15}\ \dfrac{}{12}\ \dfrac{}{11}\ \dfrac{}{13}\qquad \dfrac{}{7}\ \dfrac{}{12}\ \dfrac{}{6}$

$\dfrac{}{2}\ \dfrac{}{4}\ \dfrac{}{8}\ \dfrac{}{14}\qquad$ Y $\dfrac{}{4}\ \dfrac{}{3}\ \dfrac{}{8}$

$\dfrac{}{9}\ \dfrac{}{4}\ \dfrac{}{14}$. ' "

To discover a key phrase that Jesus said, solve the problems below to find the missing letters.

M	R	I	U	T	L	S
5+5=	2+6=	7+4=	1+2=	3+4=	2+0=	11+4=

O	W	E	P	H	D	G
3+1=	2+3=	4+2=	7+6=	8+4=	5+9=	3+6=

Prayer

Dear God,
When I am tempted to do bad things, please help me to be strong. Thank you that you understand my temptations. Please give me the strength to say no every time I am tempted to sin. Amen.

Bonus

Have each member of your family draw a picture of someone being tempted to do something wrong. Discuss what is happening in your pictures. Then give ideas about how someone could win over the temptation and make the right choice.

11

Herod Kills John the Baptist

Sometimes it is hard to listen when people correct us. Even if we know they are right, it is hard to say, "I'm wrong."

John the Baptist taught others to follow Jesus. He was not afraid to say what was good and what was bad, even about the king. King Herod had been living with his brother's wife, Herodias, as if they were married. Herod could have listened to John and changed his ways. But instead, he made a terrible choice.

Bible Reading

[4]Herod arrested John because he told Herod: "It is not right for you to have Herodias." [5]Herod wanted to kill John, but he was afraid of the people. They believed that John was a prophet. [6]On Herod's birthday, the daughter of Herodias danced for Herod and his guests. Herod was very pleased with her, [7]so he promised he would give her anything she wanted. [8]Herodias told her daughter what to ask for. So she said to Herod, "Give me the head of John the Baptist here on a platter." [9]King Herod was very sad. But he had promised to give her anything she wanted, and the people eating with him had heard his promise. So Herod ordered that what she asked for be done. (Matthew 14:4-9)

You can discover more about John the Baptist by reading Matthew 3:1-17 and Matthew 14:1-12.

Discussion

1. When was a time someone said to you, "I was wrong—please forgive me," or "I'm sorry"?

2. Why did Herod arrest John (verse 4)?

3. What did the people believe about John the Baptist (verse 5)?

4. If Herod was king, why was he afraid of the people?

5. How do you feel when someone tells you you are doing wrong?

✎6. Why did Herod decide to keep his promise to Herodias's daughter (verse 9)?

7. What are some good answers to choose when someone corrects you?

4. The relationship of rulers to the people they rule may be difficult for young children to grasp. This could be an opportunity, however, to develop the idea that citizens can make a difference by expressing their opinions. Even a totalitarian ruler with the power of Herod had to worry about public opinion.

6. For older children, this is an excellent case study of the power of peer pressure or the opinions of others. Herod may not have felt that it was a wise choice, but he was too concerned about his reputation, within the family as well as the kingdom.

7. This may or may not lead to discussion of specific incidents in recent family life. While it is not desirable for children to simply parrot "I'm sorry" whenever they are corrected, the story of Herod might help them understand that correction is meant for their own good.

Activity

Herod had a choice. Rearrange the words according to the symbols provided to find a choice that Herod should have made.

Prayer

Dear God,
Sometimes it hurts for me to be told I'm wrong. Please help me
to listen to the people who correct me, because they love me.
Thank you for parents and friends who help me avoid bad
choices.
In Jesus' name, amen.

Bonus

Play a game of pretend with a grownup. The grownup will
pretend that he or she is doing something bad. Your job is to
correct him or her and explain why this is wrong. Then the
grownup has a chance to make a good choice about how to
answer the correction.

12

Peter's Mistake

Imagine you are in the middle of a long bridge over a wide river. You see a beautiful scene—tree-covered hills in the distance, a gently curving river and a deer getting a drink. But then you look down and see how far it is to the water and how there's nothing under you but the bridge.

When Peter and the other followers were in a boat during a storm and Jesus came walking on the water, Peter thought that he wanted to walk on the water, too. At first he was fine, but when he started thinking about the dangers instead of Jesus' power and love for him, he started to sink. Choosing to keep our thoughts on Jesus is part of what it means to have faith.

Bible Reading

[25]Between three and six o'clock in the morning, Jesus' followers were still in the boat. Jesus came to them. He was walking on the water. [26]When the followers saw him walking on the water, they were afraid. They said, "It's a ghost!" and cried out in fear.

[27]But Jesus quickly spoke to them. He said, "Have courage! It is I! Don't be afraid."

[28]Peter said, "Lord, if that is really you, then tell me to come to you on the water."

²⁹Jesus said, "Come."

And Peter left the boat and walked on the water to Jesus. ³⁰But when Peter saw the wind and the waves, he became afraid and began to sink. He shouted, "Lord, save me!"

³¹Then Jesus reached out his hand and caught Peter. Jesus said, "Your faith is small. Why did you doubt?" (Matthew 14:25-31)

Discussion

1. What made Jesus' followers in the boat afraid (verse 26)?

2. How did Jesus react when Peter wanted to walk on the water (verse 29)?

3. What happened when Peter saw the wind and waves (verse 30)?

4. How can thinking about Jesus help you when you are scared?

5. How can you grow in the kind of faith that let Jesus walk on water?

✎6. When you are afraid, what do you sometimes worry about?

6. This question is phrased very generally, but your child is likely to gravitate toward a situation which is currently frightening to him or her. For instance, if your child is going through a fear of the dark, he or she may tell you about monsters imagined when the lights go out. A discussion like this, at some distance from the frightening circumstance, could be a good opportunity to talk about prayer as an antidote to those thoughts and worries that tend to magnify our fears.

✎7. Why is it easy for us to forget how Jesus can help us?

Activity

A B C D E F G̷ H I J K L M N O P Q̷ R S T U V W X̷ X Y Z̷

MOR__ING   LOR __

STI__L   __ETER

__ OAT   LE__T

__ ESUS   WAL__ED

__ INK   W__ND

W__TER   __ AVES

AF__AID   S__OUTED

GHOS__   SA__E

F__AR   CO__E

SP__KE   __OU

CO__RAGE   O'__LOCK

Use the alphabet above to complete the words that are listed. Letters that do not appear are already crossed off. Hint: All the words above appear in the Bible reading.

Prayer

Dear God,
You know that I can make my fears worse by worrying. Thank you that you love me. Thank you that you are always ready to reach out and help me. Help me to keep my thoughts on you, especially when I am afraid.
In Jesus' name, amen.

Explain as this is going on that as we walk by faith, we have to trust the Lord to lead us, even if we do not know where we are being led. Your youngest child might especially enjoy being the first leader. Stay away from stairs for safety.

Bonus

To get an idea of what it means to walk by faith, blindfold each member of your family except for one person, who will be the guide. Have everyone hold hands and ask the guide to lead the rest of the family around the house. The people with blindfolds now have to trust the guide not to lead them into walls or dangerous places. A careful guide will be able to take the rest of the family safely through the house. Take turns, allowing each family member a chance to guide.

13

Pilate Follows the Crowd

Allow your child to answer the questions.

Did anyone ever talk you into doing something you really didn't want to do? How did you feel after you did it?

A governor named Pilate had to make an important decision one day about Jesus. Some people wanted Jesus punished. In his heart, Pilate knew the right thing to do. He knew that Jesus hadn't done anything wrong, and he should let him go. But he listened to the crowd instead.

Bible Reading

[22]Pilate asked, "What should I do with Jesus, the one called the Christ?"

They all answered, "Kill him on a cross!"

[23]Pilate asked, "Why do you want me to kill him? What wrong has he done?"

But they shouted louder, "Kill him on a cross!"

[24]Pilate saw that he could do nothing about this, and a riot was starting. So he took some water and washed his hands in front of the crowd. Then he said, "I am not guilty of this man's death. You are the ones who are causing it!"

[25]All the people answered, "We will be responsible. We accept for ourselves and for our children any punishment for his death."

To learn more about Pilate, read Matthew 27:11-26 together.

²⁶Then Pilate freed Barabbas. Pilate told some of the soldiers to beat Jesus with whips. Then he gave Jesus to the soldiers to be killed on a cross. (Matthew 27:22-26)

Discussion

1. What did Pilate ask the people (verse 22)?

2. What did the people want Pilate to do with Jesus? (verses 22-23)

3. What did Pilate want to show by washing his hands (verse 24)?

✎4. Was Pilate really not guilty, just because he washed his hands?

4. This question might lead to an interesting discussion of excuses that people make for their actions. At one time or another, all of us want to blame someone else for our own mistakes. Help your child to apply this concept to his or her own life.

5. What does it mean to follow the crowd?

6. Why should we be careful about who we listen to?

✎7. What should you do if someone asks you do to something which is not right?

Activity

One of these bunches of grapes has chosen not to go along with the crowd.
Find the one that has no match.

Prayer

Dear God,
Help me to welcome your Holy Spirit in my heart and to learn the Bible so I will know what is right. When I do know what is right, help me to do it, even if others tell me to do something else. If I am with other kids who might get me into trouble, please give me the courage to say no and to leave them.
In Jesus' name, amen.

Bonus

Ask your parent to make up the beginning of a story about you and some other people. It should be a story where you have to choose to do the right thing. Then *you* finish the story. See if you would know how to make a good choice. Then talk about why that choice would be hard and how you could be brave enough to do it.

In making up your story, try to choose a situation which is clearly hypothetical, yet not too far from the child's realm of experience. You might want to start with a relatively transparent situation, and then pose a more complicated or difficult one as the child gains confidence. If other family members are available, you might ask them to make up a scenario, or make one up for them to answer.

14

Four Fishermen Follow Jesus

Fishing can be fun. But sometimes it's very boring. You put the line in the water and wait and wait. Nothing happens. Then one day you catch a fish and it's very exciting.

Jesus offered a very important choice to some fishermen one day. It is the same choice he gives to you and me and every person. He wants us to follow him. If we do, we have the joy of knowing Jesus and the gift of eternal life.

Bible Reading

[16]When Jesus was walking by Lake Galilee, he saw Simon and Simon's brother, Andrew. They were fishermen and were throwing a net into the lake to catch fish. [17]Jesus said to them, "Come and follow me. I will make you fishermen for me." [18]So Simon and Andrew immediately left their nets and followed him.

[19]Jesus continued walking by Lake Galilee. He saw two more brothers, James and John, the sons of Zebedee. They were in their boat, preparing their nets to catch fish. [20]Their father Zebedee and the men who worked for him were in the boat with the brothers. When Jesus saw the brothers, he called them to come with him. They left their father and followed Jesus. (Mark 1:16-20)

Discussion

1. What would you do if someone came through the door right now and said, "Stop what you're doing and come with me"?

2. What were Simon and Andrew doing when Jesus saw them (verse 16)?

3. What does it mean to be fishers for Jesus?

4. What did Simon and Andrew do after Jesus called them (verse 18)?

5. Why was this a difficult decision for the fishermen to make?

✎6. Who might have argued with James and John about their decision? Why?

✎7. Has anyone ever argued with you about your decision to believe in Jesus? What did you do?

5. These fishermen were leaving their livelihood. Once they left their fishing, they had no way of earning a living or of supporting any relatives who depended on their income.

6. Because the father and the hired workers are mentioned, they seem like logical candidates to differ with James and John. Sons in that time were expected to carry on their fathers' trades. They had probably been working with their father since they were young boys. To some people, James and John stood to lose a lot by following after Jesus of Nazareth.

7. If your child does not relate to this question, or even if he or she does, you might want to take this opportunity to share with your child about some significant instance of opposition to your own faith and how you handled it.

Activity

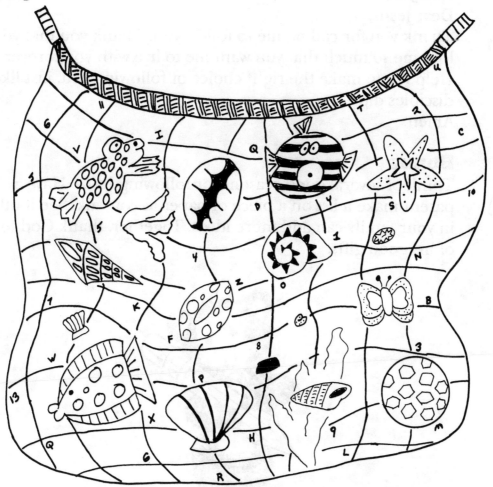

You may find many different things in a net. Draw a line between the two numbers or letters that are the same. Where they intersect, you will find what the disciples were looking for before they came to follow Christ.

Prayer

Dear Jesus,
Thank you for calling me to follow you. Thank you that you love me so much that you want me to live with you forever. Help me to make the right choice of following you, just like the disciples did.
Amen.

Bonus

Think of several good reasons for following Jesus. Have a parent make a list on a piece of paper as you talk. See if others in your family can add more ideas. Together, thank God for all of his good gifts.

15

Jairus Trusts Jesus

Allow your child to answer the questions.

Have you ever wanted something very much, but it seemed too hard or took too long, so you gave up? What happened after that?

A man named Jairus had heard that Jesus healed people. His little girl was very sick, and he wanted more than anything for her to get well. So he went to get Jesus. But on the way to Jarius's house, some men came to tell Jesus that the daughter was dead. Let's see what happened.

Bible Reading

²²A ruler from the synagogue, named Jairus, came to that place. Jairus saw Jesus and bowed before him. ²³The ruler begged Jesus again and again. He said, "My little daughter is dying. Please come and put your hands on her. Then she will be healed and will live." ²⁴So Jesus went with the ruler, and many people followed Jesus. They were pushing very close around him.

³⁵ . . . Some men came from the house of Jairus, the synagogue ruler. The men said, "Your daughter is dead. There is now no need to bother the teacher." ³⁶But Jesus paid no attention to what the men said. He said to the synagogue ruler, "Don't be afraid; only believe." . . .

⁴⁰But they only laughed at Jesus. He told all the people to

leave. Then he went into the room where the child was. He took the child's father and mother and his three followers into the room with him. [41]Then he took hold of the girl's hand and said to her, "Talitha, koum!" (This means, "Little girl, I tell you to stand up!") [42]The girl stood right up and began walking. (She was 12 years old.) (Mark 5:22-24, 35-36, 40-42)

Discussion

1. What did Jairus beg Jesus to do for his daughter (verse 23)?

2. Why did it take so long to get to Jairus's house (verse 24)?

3. What did Jesus tell Jairus to do about the bad news (verse 36)?

✎4. Why didn't Jesus pay any attention to the bad news from Jairus's house?

5. What good choice did Jairus make?

6. Why did Jesus take only a few people with him when he raised the little girl from the dead?

✎7. What can you do the next time you feel ready to give up on something important?

5. In the Gospels, there is an emphasis on the importance of faith being present when a miracle is performed. Many of the people at Jairus's house laughed when Jesus refused to act as if the child were dead. Jesus wanted people to choose to believe before he demonstrated his power. The people who witnessed this miracle believed.

6. Jesus knew that he had power over death, so he was able to remain calm in spite of the despair of the people around him.

7. This discussion will be most helpful if you encourage your child to bring up specifics from his or her life. Clearly, God does not choose to act in every "impossible" circumstance of our lives. You can begin to help your child develop the mature faith that knows that God is *able* to do miracles, but that God's purposes are often beyond our understanding.

Activity

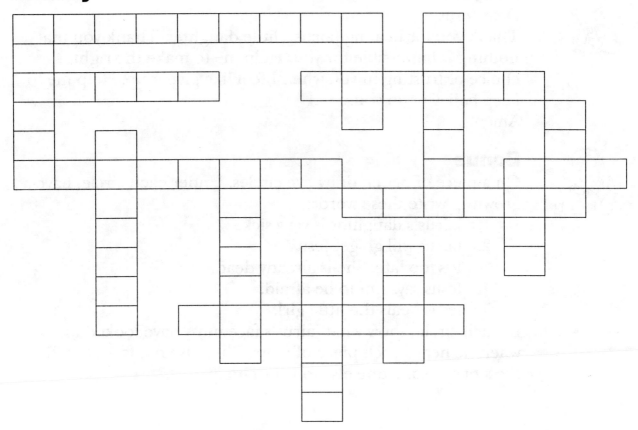

The words listed below all appear in the Bible reading. Use them to complete the diagram. Fill in the longest words first.

3 Letters	4 Letters	5 Letters	6 Letters	7 Letters	8 Letters
was	live	ruler	begged	pushing	daughter
	went		healed	believe	
	need		afraid	walking	**9 Letters**
	dead		Jairus	teacher	attention

Prayer

Dear Jesus,

Thank you for healing Jairus's little daughter. Thank you that nothing is impossible for you. Help me to make the right choice of trusting in you when I feel like giving up. Help me to keep believing in you.

Amen.

Bonus

On a piece of paper, draw five circles. Under each circle, have a grownup write these words:

1. Jairus's daughter is very sick.
2. Jairus will go get Jesus.
3. It's too late. She is already dead.
4. Jesus says not to be afraid.
5. Jesus heals the little girl.

In each circle, show what Jairus's face must have looked like when he heard each piece of news. Then use the faces to tell the story to someone else in your family.

16

A Rich Man's Reward

Allow your child to answer the question.

What is something that belongs to you that is very important to you? It could be a toy, a pet or even a coin collection. It's OK to have things you like and even love, but if this thing becomes more important to you than the Lord, you have made a bad choice.

A rich man learned that being good is not how we get to heaven. We must depend on Jesus. But if we're holding tightly to something else, we can't hold on to Jesus.

Bible Reading

[17]Jesus started to leave, but a man ran to him and fell on his knees before Jesus. The man asked, "Good teacher, what must I do to get the life that never ends?"

[18]Jesus answered, . . . [19]"You know the commands: 'You must not murder anyone. You must not be guilty of adultery. You must not steal. You must not tell lies about your neighbor in court. You must not cheat. Honor your father and mother.' "

[20]The man said, "Teacher, I have obeyed all these commands since I was a boy."

[21]Jesus looked straight at the man and loved him. Jesus said, "There is still one more thing you need to do. Go and sell everything you have, and give the money to the poor. You will have a

If your child is interested in reading the whole story of the rich young man's question, see Mark 10:17-31.

reward in heaven. Then come and follow me."
²²He was very sad to hear Jesus say this, and he left. The man was sad because he was very rich. (Mark 10:17-22)

Discussion

1. What did Jesus tell the rich man he had to do in order to get the life that never ends (verse 21)?

2. How did the rich man feel when he heard what Jesus said (verse 22)?

3. Why do you think the man was not willing to give up his riches?

✎4. How do we know what was important to the man in the story?

5. Where did Jesus say the man would find his reward (verse 21)?

6. Why doesn't Jesus want anything to get in the way of our love for him?

✎7. Besides money, what do people hang on to that keeps them from depending on Jesus?

1. Take a few moments to explain to your child that this lesson does not teach that we all must sell all our possessions before we can follow Christ; however, we must be willing to give them up if necessary. Jesus sensed the stumbling block in this particular man's life. The problem could be different for different people. However, money in some form is a stumbling block for many people.

4. When the man walked away unwilling to give his money to the poor, he showed that money was most important to him.

Activity

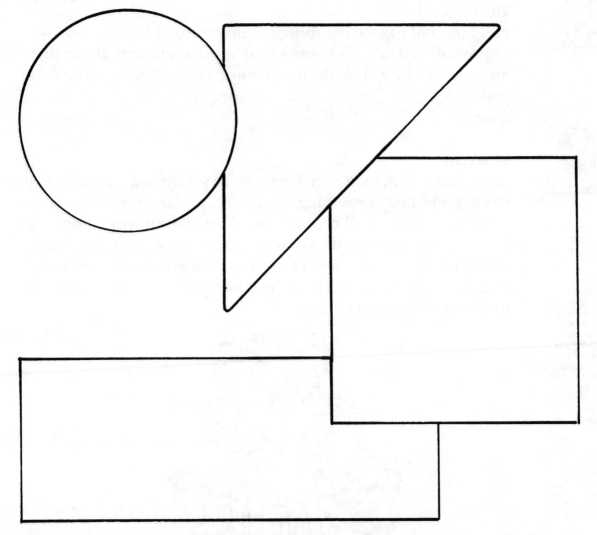

Draw four things in the shapes above that you can give to the poor.

Prayer

Dear Lord Jesus,
Help me not to love my things so much that I forget how important you are. Help me to make good choices about what and whom I love. Thank you that everything I have came from you.
Amen.

Bonus

Take time today, or sometime soon, to go through your toys or clothes and find something to give away. Make sure it is something that is still nice and would make someone else happy. This may sound easy, but once you start, you may find that even things you haven't used in a long time are special to you. Then ask your parent to help you decide on someone who needs the thing you chose.

For younger children, it may be enough to choose a younger friend or acquaintance to inherit his or her chosen possession. You may want to discourage "gifts" to siblings, since the items will still be in the house and subject to reappropriation, whether accidental or otherwise. With older children, you could find an agency that collects used items, such as a food or clothing pantry, the Salvation Army or a crisis pregnancy center. Explain the needs of the people served by that organization and, if possible, take your child with you to deliver some items. You may also want to help your child make a card that tells about the love of Jesus.

Ananias Overcomes Fear

Allow your child to respond

What if a parent or teacher told you to do something nice for somebody you always thought was mean? Would you want to do it? This is just what happened to a believer in Jesus named Ananias. God himself told Ananias to go to a man named Saul and heal him. Ananias had heard that Saul was being mean to many Christians. He had to choose whether to listen to his fears or to obey God.

Bible Reading

[10]The Lord spoke to Ananias in a vision, "Ananias!" Ananias answered, "Here I am, Lord." [11]The Lord said to him, "Get up and go to the street called Straight Street. Find the house of Judas. Ask for a man named Saul from the city of Tarsus. He is there now, praying. [12]Saul has seen a vision. In it a man named Ananias comes to him and lays his hands on him. Then he sees again." [13]But Ananias answered, "Lord, many people have told me about this man and the terrible things he did to your people in Jerusalem. [14]Now he has come here to Damascus. The leading priests have given him the power to arrest everyone who worships you." [15]But the Lord said to Ananias, "Go! I have chosen Saul for an important work. He must tell about me to

non-Jews, to kings, and to the people of Israel. [16]I will show him how much he must suffer for my name." [17]So Ananias went to the house of Judas. He laid his hands on Saul and said, "Brother Saul, the Lord Jesus sent me. He is the one you saw on the road on your way here. He sent me so that you can see again and be filled with the Holy Spirit." (Acts 9:10-17)

Discussion

1. What did the Lord tell Ananias and Paul about each other (verses 11-12)?

2. What bad things had Ananias heard about Saul (verses 13-14)?

3. Why did God want Ananias to heal Saul (verse 15)?

3. Explain that Saul had been blinded while traveling to the city of Damascus. He had been on his way to persecute Christians, but Jesus appeared to him in a bright light and took away his sight

✎4. When Ananias chose to obey God, how did he help many people besides Saul?

5. How did Ananias's choice show that he was a good friend of the Lord (verse 17)?

6. Why are Christians sometimes afraid to do what God asks?

✎7. What can you do next time you are a little afraid to do what you know to be right?

7. This is a good opportunity to discuss Jesus' command to love our enemies (Luke 6:27-31).

Activity

Lord	non-Jew	go	people of Israel
went	here	Jesus	see
Saul	am	laid	I
here	hands	Ananias	kings

Cross out the words in the chart that match the descriptions listed below. Next, write the words that are left in the blanks below to complete the sentence.

1. Three types of people that Saul is to tell about Jesus (verse 15).

2. The three characters in this Bible reading.

3. The four words that Ananias uses to answer God in verse 10.

4. Two words with two *e*'s.

God said, "_____ ." And, Ananias _____ .

He _____ his _____ on Saul.

Prayer

Dear Lord,
Thank you that you can see inside the heart of every person.
Thank you that you can change people, even people who do
terrible things. When I have a chance to do something nice for
a mean person, help me to make a good choice.
In Jesus' name, amen.

Bonus

Think of one person who has been mean to you. Then pray
with your parent that God will change that person's heart.

You may want to come
back to this passage of
Scripture from time to
time as your child en-
counters difficulties in
his or her relationships.
The act of prayer in it-
self is a way of return-
ing good for evil. And,
more importantly,
prayer has a way of
changing the hearts of
those who pray, as well.

18

Peter Accepts Cornelius

Do you tease people who are different from you? The Bible teaches that simply because someone is different, that person is no less important in the eyes of God. We are to treat people with the same amount of kindness we would like people to show us.

Peter had to learn this lesson when he went to visit Cornelius. Cornelius was not a Jew, and Peter did not have contact with anyone who was not a Jew. But God came to Peter in a vision and told him that this was wrong. After he listened to God, Peter chose to obey.

Bible Reading

²⁵When Peter entered, Cornelius met him. He fell at Peter's feet and worshiped him. ²⁶But Peter helped him up, saying, "Stand up! I too am only a man." ²⁷Peter went on talking with Cornelius as they went inside. There Peter saw many people together. ²⁸He said, "You people understand that it is against our Jewish law for a Jew to associate with or visit anyone who is not a Jew. But God has shown me that I should not call any person 'unholy' or 'unclean.' ²⁹That is why I did not argue when I was asked to come here. Now, please tell me why you sent for me." (Acts 10:25-29)

To read the whole story of Peter and Cornelius, see Acts 10:1-33.

Discussion

1. What did Cornelius do when he met Peter (verse 25)?

2. What had God shown Peter (verse 28)?

1. You will probably need to explain that Cornelius had such high regard for Peter that he was actually worshiping Peter like God. Peter had to correct him. Cornelius's attitude is in sharp contrast to the disdain of the Jews, who wouldn't even associate with these Gentiles.

3. How should we treat all people?

4. Why do people sometimes tease or hurt others because they are different?

4. Be sensitive to the fact that your own child may be teased for some reason, even if this is not apparent to you. Let him or her talk about how this feels. Reassure your child that God loves him/her very much and is not pleased when others are unkind.

5. Do you know someone who often gets teased? If so, how can you be more kind to that person?

5. For most children, the dilemma of the scapegoat is not that they want to be cruel, but that they are afraid of risking the same scorn from their peers if they stick up for someone else.

✎6. What does the word *prejudice* mean?

Why did God want Peter to give up his prejudice against the Gentiles?

✎7. Why is it good for us to have many friends who are different from us?

Activity

W 🐔 Peter entered, 🌽elius met him. He fell at Peter's 👣 and wor🚤ed him. But Peter helped him up, saying, "Stand up! 👁2️⃣ am only a man." Peter w🐔t on tal👑 with 🌽elius as th🍃 w🐔t inside. Th🐰 Peter 🐛 many 🫛ple together. He said, ..."God has shown me that 👁 should 🌰 call any person 'un🧀' or 'unclean.'"

This is the Bible reading with symbols replacing certain words. Without peeking at the Bible reading, try to figure out what the symbols mean.

Prayer

Dear God,
Please help me to be kind and courteous to others. When I meet someone who is different from me, please help me to accept that person, even if he or she does not accept me.
In Jesus' name, amen.

Bonus

As a family, talk about different types of people who are teased. How do these people look different? Are they short, tall, fat or skinny? Are they red, yellow, black or white-skinned? Do they have a handicap? Are they simply not good at sports? Talk about ways that you want to treat these people. See if you can think of ways to help your friends do the same.

After you talk, you may wish to end by singing "Jesus Loves the Little Children."

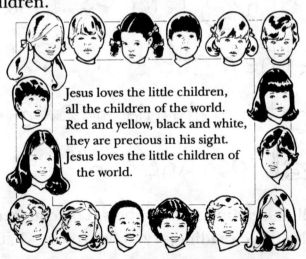

Jesus loves the little children,
all the children of the world.
Red and yellow, black and white,
they are precious in his sight.
Jesus loves the little children of
the world.